Photoshop Elements 13 For Beginners:

The Ultimate Photo Organizing, Editing, Perfecting Manual Guide For Digital Photographers

By

Joseph Joyner

Table of Contents

Photoshop Elements 13 For Beginners: The Ultimate Photo Organizing, Editing, Perfecting Manual Guide For Digital Photographers

By Joseph Joyner

Introduction

We take photos every day and we cannot deny that we love doing that. So if you are looking for a way to quickly edit your photos, synchronize it in the web and share it then you must try Photoshop Elements 13.

Sounds intimidating? Haven't tried editing your photos? Then, read the following tips and tricks described in this book to kick start your photo editing.

Chapter 1. What is Photoshop Element 13?

-Photoshop Element 13 is allows you to take, edit, create and share your photos wherever you go. It is a cheaper version of Photoshop and perfect for photographers and anyone who is on the go.

How Adobe Photoshop Element 13 can be different from Adobe Premiere Elements and Adobe?

-Adobe Photoshop Element 13 is for photographers who are on the go who wants to quickly organize, edit , create and share their photos via computer, web and mobile.

On the other hand,

-Adobe Premiere Elements is for videographers who likewise can quickly organize, edit , create and share their videos via computer, web and mobile.

And,

-Adobe Photoshop Lightroom is for beginners who just started editing their photos.

Chapter 2. What Can I Do In Photoshop Element 13?

-Crop your photos using four compositions.

-it has realistic color and lightning blend so your photos will be truthful.

-Synchronizing the photos to your mobile and web is easier and faster

-It has powerful and fun editing tools.

-There is a quick mode that will help you to edit in one click.

-You can create scrapbooks because of its layering options.

-It allows photo mail, photo merge, texture fill, Panorama and magic extractor

-Create cool digital artwork and edit graphics for websites

The 3 windows of Photoshop Elements

-Quick that enables quick mode. It contains simple tools that will help you to correct your photos, this includes lightings and red eye.

-Guided that enables guided edit mode. It contains tools for basic editing and photographic effects. If you are a newbie in photo editing, the use the guided mode.

-Expert that enables you to edit in expert mode. It allows advance editing and correction of color problems, special effects and photo enchantment.

The Workspace

Just like any other editing software Adobe Photoshop has the same workspace.

1. Menu bar, where the entire menu is located to perform the task.

2. Toolbox, where tools are located for editing your photos.

3. Taskbar, where the frequently used actions are displayed such as the buttons for quick and easy access.

4. Mode selector, where buttons of the 3 mode can be viewed.

5. Panel bin, where feature, actions and controls are grouped.

What Are Mobile Albums?

-Mobile Albums allow you to your photos that are saved in your computer or even in the web. By this you can have your computer wherever you go.

Chapter 3. Quick Photoshop Element 13 Tutorial

Content Aware

-This allows you to clean the surrounding of your image. Example you want to remove a delete a part in your background, you can use this,

-use the Lasso tool to select the photo, Go to the menu, click edit > fill selection. From the use list, choose content aware fill and elements that will automatically fill the chosen area.

-It allows to fill it with a color that matches the area so your photo will be edited seamlessly.

-You can also try making slightly different selection and then use Content Aware fill and you will see how different and uniquely it works.

Quick Edit Effects

-this allows you to have edict quickly by using a preset effect. You can look at the right side to choose one.

Auto Crop Suggestion

-This allows you to have suggestions when cropping a photo. You can still crop it like the traditional way of cropping, but it allows you have better suggestions to try.

Effects Panel

- If you are into presets and effects then you can check the effects panel in the expert edit mode. You will see the different effects by categories.

New Guided Edits

-Guided edit mode, allows you to have more control over your effects. They are categorized in a little different way, here the camera effect and photo effect are separated from each other.

Refine Selection Brush

-This allows your selections to go along after you created them. You can use this to make refine selection which is a must try.

Facebook Cover Photo

-Creating a facebook cover in Adobe Photoshop Element 13 is fun. It is in the right side so you can be sure that "what you see is what you get" when you apply the photo in the header.

-Go to the create tab and choose facebook cover and this will directs you to basics or advanced mode.

Photo Merge Compose

-This option allows you to move people from one photo to another. Example, you have taken a family photo and your brother is not there, you can use this photo to bring new people and change the background in the photo.

-Just click enhance then photomerge compose and this will direct you up a screen commanding you to place the photo with the people you want to extract first. It has also have a refine edge option to make it seamless.

eLive Option

-eLive is a way to include tutorials and news right in the Elements app, without you having to go on the web search to look for it. Look at it at the Organizer or maybe in the editor at the very top.

Expert Mode Effects

-It is a smart way to edit your picture with its newly categorized revised effects in the effects panel. There are over new 19 effects and you can see the thumbnails for reference while you are editing.

History Panel

While editing your photos, the history panel can be your guide. It allows you to jump to any recent state of the image that you created during your editing.

To cancel an operation you can also Undo, redo or cancel it. Just go to the Edit and the click either Undo or Redo.

Note that it lists the 50 previous operations, beyond that are deleted to space memory for Photoshop elements.

More About Quick Mode

-Quick mode groups the basic photo-fixing tools in one place. It allows you to quickly fix the exposure , color and more. You can see this in the Adjustments panel and each of the panels has a live preview.

-There are over 10 available effects where each has five variations. You can transform your photo by applying the effect by clicking thumbnails. It ranges from Black and white effects to different vintage effects.

-When you choose an effect, this will be visible as a new layer mask. Then you can also click the expert mode to edit the layer. You can either remove or reduce the effect.

-To edit the texture, go to the texture panel and choose from the10 available texture. Examples of textures are old paper, chrome feel, rough blue grid and cracked paint texture.

-You can use the frames panel to add frames. It is automatically fitted in your photo in the best way possible. Just double click the frame to apply and if you wish to modify it, you can switch to expert mode and click color fill layer.

Steps to Apply an Effect, Texture and Frame in Photoshop Elements 13

1. Make sure that your photo is open in the workspace.

2. Switch to quick mode.

3. Go to 3 panels and apply your chosen effects, textures and frames that is available in the adjustment panel.

4. Switch to expert mode to modify the effect, texture and frame. This is available in separate layers so click the ones you want to edit.

How to Fit an Image in The Screen?

1. To fir it, double-click the hand tool in the toolbox.

2. Or select a zoom tool or the hand tool, then click fit screen button that you can see in the tool options bar.

3. Choose view then click Fit On Screen.

How to Manage Your Workflow?

-Click an item in the library to select a preset.

-In saving a brush, click open in the pop-up panel and pick Save Brush command, after that input a name into the dialog box.

-To delete a brush, select an item, open the pop-up panel in the menu, and click the delete command. To load it, follow the same instruction and then select load.

-To add assets to an existing library, then click Append. On the other hand, to replace the current set of your brushes, open the pop-up panel menu, then select a new one.

How to Use The Preset Manager?

-Expert mode enables you to create a set of favorite brushes. Just click Expert mode, in the edit click Preset Manager and manage the brushes, colors, gradients, styles, effects, patterns and swatches.

-From there, you can load a library. Click the Preset Manager, and then choose brushes, gradients, swatches, patterns, style, and effects.

- You can click "reset", restores the default library.

-To rename a preset, select a preset in the list and click rename or just simply double-click a present.

Chapter 4. File Management

How to Import Files?

-To import files, choose file, click import.

-Choose a specific destination in which the files will be saved on your computer.

-Make sure that OAI or Open Acquired Image is selected to facilitate importing large number of files.

-Using date today, to select create unique subfolder to save the imported images directly into a folder.

-After all of these, you can now click "start".

-Select the digital camera and the images you want to import.

-To finally import the images, then click get pictures.

Guide to Managing Your Files

1. Opening the files

-Adobe Photoshop Elements gives you choice about working in your files. This will help you optimize and combine files easier.

-Create a blank file in your workspace and open a previous used file and specify which to open.

How to change the display of items in a pop-up panel menu?

1. Change the display of one panel by opening the pop-up panel menu. Click the menu icon in the upper-right corner.

-To change the display of all your panels, you can click Edit > Preset Manager to open the preset manager, and from there click the more button.

2. You can also select the view options.

a. The "text only" displays the name of each item.

b. The "small or large thumbnail" displays the respected thumbnail of each item.

c. The "Large list or small list" shows the name and thumbnails of every item.

e. The "Stroke thumbnail" is where the brush thumbnail and sample brush stroke are displayed.

Chapter 5. Editing

1. Create a new blank file.

Example: If you want to make a graphic, logo or a banner, you need to make it in a blank file.

Here is a step by step tutorial to do it.

a. Click File > New > Blank File.

b. Enter your chosen options then click

OK.

a. Name: to name the new image file.

b. Preset: to set the width, height and resolution of images that you want to use and see on the screen.

c. Size: there are standard sizes that are listed and you can choose from them.

d. Color mode: this allows you to set the image in RGB, grayscale, CMYK or bitmap.

f. Background Contents: It sets the color of the background image. The default color is white, but you can change it. You have to select Background Color to use by clicking in the color that is shown in the toolbox.

How to Set The Color Modes?

-In the info panel, choose a color mode:

a. Grayscale: It shows grayscale values below the pointer.

b. Web color: It shows hexadecimal code of the RGB color.

c. RGB color: It displays the RGB values (Red, Green and Blue)

How to Change The Information in The Info Panel?

The information displayed in the Info panel or status bar can be changed by:

1. Go to the info panel and choose Panel Options from the more options of the menu bar.

2. After that select a view option.

a. " Document sizes " is the size of the printing size of the image which you can see written in the left side.

For the numbers indicated in the right side is the approximate size of the files including the layers.

b. " Document Profile " exhibits the name of your file.

c. " Document Dimensions " shows the size of the currently selected items or units.

d. " Scratch Size " is the RAM and scratch disk space used to process the image.

e. " Efficiency " is the time spent in applying an operation. If you can see that the value is 1005 which is written below. Then it means that Adobe Photoshop Elements is utilizing the scratch disk and can your operation slower.

f. " Timing " this shows how long it procured to finish the last operation.

g. " Current Tool " displays the name of the active tool that you are currently using.

How to Adjust The Color, Saturation and Hue?

-Use the slider of the hue to add effects, for example you can add " sepia effect ".

-Use the slider of saturation to make colors vivid or muted. For example, adding a color punch to a photo by saturating it. You can also tone down a color that you find disturbing.

Step by step tutorial:

1. Click Enhance, then choose Adjust color and then adjust the hue and saturation.

2. You can also click a specific layer, the click new adjustment layer and click hue and saturation.

3. Click the edit tab and choose which color you want to adjust. To adjust all colors at once, you can click Master.

4. You can also click the slider and enter a value of color. Note that the colors exhibited are shades of color that is near the original color.

5. For the hue, values are from - 180 to + 180. For the saturation, values are from - 100 to + 100.

6. Adjusting the lightness, you can drag the slider to the right to increase the saturation or left to decrease it. You can also put a value ranging from – 100 to+ 100.

7. Don't forget to click the OK button if you are done or the cancel button to repeat again.

8. You can also lighten or darken a portion of your image by using the other adjustments options.

Basic Editing Tutorial

EXAMPLE 1: How to adjust the color of the skin tone.

1. You can simply adjust the entire color of the photo to achieve a more natural skin tones.

2. Tip: Separately adjust the red and brown color to achieve a natural skin tone.

3. To do this, please follow the instructions below:

a. Open the photo that you want to edit and select the layer that requires corrections and adjustments.

b. Click Enhance, the select adjust color, and then adjust the color for the skin tone.

c. If you want to only adjust a portion in the skin. Click that area and Photoshop elements will automatically adjust it, though it may be elusive.

d. Always use the preview while adjusting so you can track the changes that you apply.

f. Quick Tip: To achieve a tan skin tone, increase or decrease the level of color brown. For the blush, adjust the level of red color and adjust the overall color to manage the temperature.

g. When you achieved your desired tone, click OK. Or if not, click Cancel and begin again.

How to Convert a Photo to Black and White?

-Click the Black and White command to choose a specific type to convert your photo in black and white.

Step by Step Tutorial For Black and White Conversion

-Launch your image and select the area you wish to convert. Always make a duplicate layer when converting so you can still have a copy of the original photo once you don't like the result.

-Click Enhance the choose Convert to Black and White.

-You can also select a style option. Examples are Portraits or Landscapes.

-From the slider you can drag the level of red, blue and green to make a contrast.

-After you finalize the mode, you can now finally click OK.

-Another way to convert the photo to Black and white, you can set the saturation to − 100 in the saturation dialog box.

-For selected area in the photo, you can select it using one of the selection tool. Then click Enhance > Adjust Color > Remove Color.

How to Change The Size of The Canvas?

-To change the size of the canvas or your workspace.

1. Click Image and then click resize and click canvas size.

2. Adjust the width, height and resolution in the dialog box.

3. Click the arrow on the Anchor icon to position the image to the new canvass.

How to Add Color to a Grayscale Image?

-To add color to a grayscale image or a portion of it follow the instructions below.

Example 1; A grayscale photo of a girl with an umbrella and you want to put a color in the umbrella.

1. Click Enhance, Adjust the hue and saturation.

2. Click Enhance, then new adjustment layer and adjust the Hue and Saturation.

3. You can also select Colorize. Put a color in the foreground so Photoshop Elements 13 will adjust it.

4. Also, you can simply use the slider to select a new color if desired.

5. Click OK.

How to Fix Distorted Photos?

-To correct a distorted photo, you have to use the perspective control.

1. First is to use the rotate image or fix perspective.

2. You can also use the image grid for a more accurate correction.

a. Go to filter and select correct camera distortion.

b. Then select the preview tab to check.

c. Set your image for correction here are the different settings.

a. Remove Distortion: It corrects the lens. Just input a number in the box to bend and center the image.

b. Vignette Amount: It sets the amount of lightness and darkness from the edges of the image. The Vignette Midpoint specifies the width of the area that is affected and the Vignette Perspective corrects the image perspective.

c. Vertical and Horizontal Perspective: this corrects the image that is caused by the up and down tilting of the camera.

d. Angle: this rotates the image and corrects it.

e. scale: this adjusts the scale of the image. Just choose between up or down.

f. Grid: Clicking this show and hides the grid.

g. Color: This option specifies the color of the grid that you will use.

Guide in Retouching and correcting a Photo

Example 1: How to remove a red eye?

-Simply use the Red Eye Tool to remove the red eye. Select the automatically fix red eyes in the get photos dialog box.

-Step by step manually removing the red eye.

1. Select the "Red eye Removal" tool.

2. Select the red area in the eyes.

3. Make a selection over the area of the eye.

4. Remove the red from the eyes through releasing the mouse button.

Trivia: Red eye is the cause of illumination of the retina by the flash of the camera.

How to Remove Spots and Imperfection in The Face?

-To remove imperfection such as dark spots and pimples in the photo, you can use the healing brush tool.

1. Select the healing brush tool and choose the appropriate size of the brush.

2. In the tool options bar, choose either of the following:

a. Proximity match: This is a method where the pixels of the edge are used. You can also click edit and create texture.

b. To achieve a finer look, create a texture and use all the pixels in the selection. Drag through the area until you achieve your desired texture.

How to Remove Unwanted Objects in Your Photo?

-Example, if you have a photo in the garden and there is a garbage can near you and you want to delete it, here is how to do it.

1. Use content aware to remove the unwanted objects or figures.

2 Use the Content Aware option along with Spot Healing Brush tool to make it seamless.

Here is The Step by Step Tutorial

1. Click the spot healing brush and select Content Aware in the tool Options bar.

2. After that, you have to paint over the object or figure that you want to remove.

Note: This method is perfect if you are working in a small object. If you have a big object or figure you want to remove then try the following instead.

1. You have to draw small brush strokes at a time in the area.

Different Settings of Healing brush:

a. Mode: It determines how the pattern blends with the existing image.

b. Source: This sets the source that is used for repairing the pixels of the image.

c. Aligned: You have to deselect "Aligned" to continue using the sampled pixels.

d. Sample All layers: By choosing this option, the current layers of the photo will be visible.

3. Click the sample by positioning the pointer in any open image and the press ALT.

4. Next is to drag the image over the imperfection to blend exiting data with sampled data.

How to Clone Images or Areas in Your Photo?

-To copy or clone a specific area in your photo. Here is how you can do it.

1. Launch the photo that you will edit and select the clone stamp tool.

2. This is optional, but you can set the settings of the clone tool.

(Brush, sample all layers, opacity, size, mode and aligned)

3. After you choose the clone stamp tool, you have to click Clone overlay and set the settings.

Here is The Guide

a. Show Overlay, this allows you to view the overlay inside the brush size.

b. Opacity is to set the opacity or visibility of the overlay.

c. Clipped is to allow you to clip to the brush.

d. Auto Hide is to enable you to hide the overlay while you are working in your paint strokes.

e. Invert Overlay will allow you to invert the colors.

4. After choosing your desired setting, you have to position your pointer to the part of any open image that you wish to sample.

5. Press ALT and then click. The tool will be duplicated and the pixels at the sample.

6. Finally, drag or click to paint the image with the tool

Quick guide to Cropping an Image

To successfully crop an image, follow the instructions below.

1. Select the crop tool and then select the cropping guide that you want. (This can be the rule of thirds, golden ratio or none)

2. Then you have to drag over the part of the image that you want to remain. Release the mouse button to see the changes.

3. Click the green commit button at the lower right corner.

And there you go.

Keyboard shortcuts for fast editing

This shortcut applies to both Windows and Mac OS

P for background brush

B for Foreground brush

H for hand tool

Z for zoom tool

A for Add to selection tool

E for eraser

D for removing the selection tool

CTL + N for new blank document

CTL + O to open

CTRL + S to save your work

Note: The new feature of Photoshop elements 13 includes the 64-bit installation.

Conclusion

So if you are serious about transforming your photographs, Photoshop Elements 13 can be your partner. Aside from it is easy and quick, there are lots of options and effects to transform your boring photos in a creative one.

So better try it now and make your photos that are not only memorable, but also beautiful.

www.ingramcontent.com/pod-product-compliance
Lightning Source LLC
Chambersburg PA
CBHW051747050726
47598CB00003B/1367